Mesa Arch is one of the premier sights in the Island in the Sky section of Canyonlands National Park near Moab, Utah. The arch is perfectly placed to provide a "frame" for the photogenic sprawl of the White Rim below. Those who visit the arch at sunrise are treated to a spectacular play of color, when the ceiling of the arch is illuminated with the rosy glow of morning light reflected off the red-orange rock underneath. The scene is a dramatic one, but the hike to it needn't be; it's a half-mile round-trip on a well-marked and maintained trail.

Sandstone *to* SUMMIT

Colorado and Utah landscapes through
the lens of Christopher Tomlinson

By Dave Haynes

12/2014

Happy Trails!

Christopher
Tomlinson

THE DAILY SENTINEL
GRAND JUNCTION, COLORADO

Grand Junction Media Inc.
The Daily Sentinel
734 S. Seventh St.
Grand Junction, CO 81501
Tel: (970) 242-5050
www.GJSentinel.com

Edited by Laurena Mayne Davis
Cover and interior design by Robert García
ISBN 978-0-9889069-1-4

Cover photo: Fisher Towers along the Colorado River with La Sal mountain range in the distance.
Inside front cover: Independence Monument stands alone in this aerial view of Wedding Canyon in Colorado National Monument.
Inside back cover: The Palisade near Gateway and the La Sal Mountains of eastern Utah on the horizon.
Back cover photo: Jeff Cook hangs out in the cliffs and crags of Bangs Canyon south of Grand Junction.

Contents

Foreword   V

Introduction   VII

About the photographer   IX

About the author   XI

Chapter 1: Desert   1

Chapter 2: Petroglyphs   23

Chapter 3: Mountains   37

Chapter 4: Water   57

Chapter 5: Night sky   71

The bloom of columbines announces the arrival of summer to the San Juan Mountains of southwest Colorado. The Rocky Mountain columbine is the state flower of Colorado. Its colors represent blue skies, white snow and the gold found in Colorado's mountains.

Foreword

This book will inspire the viewer's heart while delighting the eye. Readers of The Grand Junction Daily Sentinel can count on opening their newspaper every morning and seeing Christopher Tomlinson's outstanding photojournalism on the pages. But it's those Monday photos of climbers scaling mountain passes or hikers among the hoodoos that make many exclaim, "Chris and his friends must have gone on another outdoor adventure!"

While readers might not have laced up hiking boots with Chris and friends, the breathtaking outdoor photography is a satisfying substitute.

It's the Tomlinson Touch — the ability to frame and preserve natural beauty from the blazing Comet Hale-Bopp spotted through a sandstone arch to the golden brilliance of aspen leaves against a bluebird sky in fall. The

photos in *Sandstone to Summit* are a stunning visual travelogue.

What newspaper readers may not know is that many of the paper's cutlines — the short stories below the photos — are written by Chris' friend, fellow adventurer and colleague, Dave Haynes.

Dave joins Chris here, unspooling the stories behind the photos in a clever and insightful way. For example, Dave explains why stars appear to swirl above a campsite or how a great blue heron scored a free lunch from an ice fisherman.

Chris and Dave are a winning team in *Sandstone to Summit*, leading us from sandy desert floor to thin-aired mountaintop. Turn the page and let's explore.

Tilman "Tillie" Bishop,
Former Colorado State Senator

Opposite page — Mount Sneffels dominates the skyline as you approach the San Juan Range from the north. At 14,150 feet, Sneffels is not the tallest mountain in Colorado; wearing a light dusting of snow, and ringed by golden aspens on a flawless autumn day, it is surely the most inspiring.

Introduction

By Robert García

Sandstone to Summit goes beyond the iconic, must-photograph scenery of Colorado and Utah. It is not a guide for "how to get there" or "how to get the shot," but is a collection of often-playful images that reveal human interaction with the landscape.

The inclusion of people in many of the photographs creates that personal connection — whether it is someone dwarfed by the magnitude of standing atop a 14,000-foot peak or a telltale shoeprint in the snow.

Photographer Christopher Tomlinson has willingly, faithfully and with much enthusiasm ventured out to preserve these moments in time. He has trained his eye to look beyond the obvious and to see shapes and light in order to create a balance that lends itself to striking imagery.

Dave Haynes has accompanied Chris on many of these adventures. He is able to add in an artful way the situations or circumstances behind the photographs. Together they share decades of memories, visually and verbally, of some of the most inspiring places on the planet.

The scenic vistas captured in this book are more than just places; they are an experience that is constantly changing, from day to night and from season to season.

Areas depicted include portions of the Western Slope of Colorado's Rocky Mountains and the high desert of the Colorado Plateau, which takes in western Colorado, northwestern New Mexico, southern and eastern Utah and northern Arizona. Many of Colorado's 14,000-foot mountains can be found in the San Juan Mountain range. The Colorado Plateau lays claim to 10 national parks and a dozen national monuments.

Photo by Dolores Pitman

Chapters are divided by five aspects of the landscape: Desert, Petroglyphs, Mountains, Water and Night sky. *Sandstone to Summit* is a splendid compilation of the quality and scope of Chris Tomlinson's creative accomplishments.

Ultimately, each photograph transports viewers to a place they wish they could be.

Opposite page — Dave Haynes and his dog, Molly, are frequent visitors to Fisher Towers, 16 miles northeast of Moab on Utah Highway 128. The elaborate maze of rock fins draws casual hikers and sightseers, as well as "rock jocks" who embrace the challenge of testing their climbing skills on vertical walls.

Photo by Katherine Lopez

About the photographer

Christopher "Chris" Tomlinson has photographed exceptional events: Pope John Paul II at World Youth Day and two Denver Broncos Super Bowls.

But the career newspaper photojournalist often finds his greatest inspiration far away from the news-making crowds, in the wilds of western Colorado and eastern Utah, hiking and camping with friends.

Known for his jaw-dropping landscapes, Chris is self-trained, turning a childhood curiosity with cameras into a three-decades-and-counting career. He's been lauded with dozens of state and national awards and his work has been featured in the books *Grand Junction & The Grand Valley: Visions of the 21st Century, and Monumental Majesty: 100 Years of Colorado National Monument.*

A Baltimore native, Chris found his way to western Colorado in 1982 and proclaimed it home. The only time this move has caused him cognitive dissonance is when the Denver Broncos play the Baltimore Ravens.

I have been blessed.

I'm blessed to live in a town I love and to have a job I love. Thirty-one years of making pictures for a living has been amazing. I have been invited into your homes to share in the births of babies and the deaths of loved ones. To share in your victories and the defeats at sporting events. To be on the sidelines of two Broncos Super Bowl victories. To have worked at two Olympic Games. And for the day-to-day job of making pictures for a living. I have been blessed.

I would like to thank Stan and Ginny Citko for introducing me to the Grand Valley in the early '70s, and for supporting me in my dream of becoming a photographer. Thanks, Mom and Dad.

Thanks to my family for all the love and support. To the best brothers, Terry and Jim, and my sister, Kathy, for everything a brother could ask for.

And thanks to an All-Star team in putting this book together. Thanks to Laurena Mayne Davis for her coordinating and editing skills. Thanks to my other brothers — Robert García for his great layout and design work, and to Dave Haynes for writing this book. Thank you both for years of friendship.

I would like to dedicate my work on this book to my Mom and Dad. I have been blessed. — Christopher Tomlinson

Opposite page — Wild animals often want nothing to do with two-legged interlopers, but these mountain goats in Chicago Basin, in the south San Juan Mountains, seemed as curious about humans as the humans were about them. "I thought a bunch of people brought their dogs with them," Chris said. "They weren't shy." As he got closer and saw the animals were goats, he wished he'd brought a telephoto lens. As it turned out, he only needed the wide-angle.

About the author

Colorado native Dave Haynes has scaled all 54 of the state's 14,000-foot peaks. Years of trail time in western Colorado and eastern Utah have taken him over hill and dale, nook and cranny, cliff and canyon, while dodging lightning, hailstorms and the occasional grouchy mountain goat.

Friend and colleague Christopher Tomlinson has been along on many, if not most, of these adventures since they began exploring the rugged West together a quarter-century ago. Trusty sidekick Molly, an Australian Shepherd, is a seasoned adventurer, too. Try and spot her in the pages to follow.

Dave is the news editor for *The Grand Junction Daily Sentinel.* He's worked 25 years in newspapers as a reporter, photographer and editor. He excels in clever and incisive wordplay as a headline writer and has won multiple state and national awards.

Here, he brings narrative resonance to Chris' photography.

Photo by Christopher Tomlinson

*T*hanks to everyone who thought this book was a good idea. Thanks to Laurena Mayne Davis for her guidance, and thanks to Robert García and Chris Tomlinson for lending their tremendous talents to this project. And thanks to our many mutual friends, and our families, who will be thrilled and proud that we actually pulled this off. You are all an inspiration.

Opposite page — Rough Canyon is a hidden gem, tucked away in the rugged folds of rock wilderness southeast of Colorado National Monument. Rough Canyon is accessible only to hikers, but the larger Bangs Canyon area, of which Rough Canyon is a part, is a favorite of bicycle and horseback riders as well as the Jeep and ATV crowd. If any water exists in the canyons during dry months, it likely will be found in Rough Canyon.

False Kiva is tucked away in a remote and difficult to find part of Island in the Sky in Canyonlands National Park. The kiva has been shielded by a shallow cave and therefore has undergone very little physical change since it was created – but by whom? Its very name implies uncertainty about its origin, and whether it was made by ancient inhabitants or if it's a clever forgery of a more recent age.

Desert

Hot. Harsh. Barren. Parched. The word "desert" conjures images of merciless sun, bare rock and shifting sand. Life is an exception where the rule of wilderness is strictly enforced. Nature rewards the living things that adapt to this hostile realm – and punishes those that do not. The struggle for survival is illustrated here in the starkest possible terms. In spite of this, life teems in the most unlikely of places.

Desert four o'clocks abound in Chesler Park, Needles District, Canyonlands National Park. As their name implies, the flowers open in the afternoon and through the night and have an earthy fragrance.

Indian paintbrush is a common sight in the desert Southwest. Its bright blooms can be found everywhere along the sandy benches of the Colorado Plateau. Along with its ornamental value, Native American tribes of the Southwest found a variety of medicinal uses for paintbrush.

Little Wildhorse and Bell canyons, in Utah's San Rafael Swell, often are hiked together in a large loop trail. Hikers get a workout on this 8-mile round trip, but no technical expertise is required. The route winds through steep walls and slots that are, in places, barely wide enough for a person to pass through without turning sideways. Hikers occasionally will need all four limbs to get over — or under — a fallen boulder.

A crack in the rock holds allure for a seasoned explorer of the Needles District of Canyonlands National Park. These places offer not only an element of primal security, but also cool respite on a warm day; in a narrow slot canyon, little sunlight is able to reach and heat the rock on either side of the passageway.

Every deep shadow in the desert merits investigation. Some of these shadows conceal little more than a shallow recess, darkened by a water seep. Others open doorways to the desert's well-kept secrets, such as this small room hidden in the rock at Goblin Valley State Park, Utah.

A double arch, or a cave with a sunroof? If this curious feature has a name, it's unknown to the author, and doesn't appear to be marked on a map. It's situated near, and is visible from, the junction of Utah Highway 24 and Temple Mountain Road east of Goblin Valley State Park, less than a mile off the road into the park. To find it, or something of equal scenic value, investigate the desert's deep shadows.

Opposite page — Sometimes you know what you're looking for, and sometimes you only know after you've found it. The stunning view of this northern section of the San Rafael Swell, appropriately called the Little Grand Canyon, was the reward for a careful study of a topographic map. The dense, closely spaced contour lines on the map tell of a place that indeed bears a striking similarity to its more famous namesake in Arizona.

Red-tailed hawks are a common sight in the high deserts, but the sight of a big raptor leaving a branch and catching a thermal updraft can still inspire envious thoughts in the minds of earthbound life forms.

Plateau lizards, fence lizards, common sagebrush lizards: they thrive in the Southwest, and are as ubiquitous as sun and sand in the desert. This one has the right idea in terms of color, but its interpretation of texture as camouflage clearly has room to evolve.

A side of Fisher Towers that nobody sees by accident. The Top of the World trail is a rough Jeep road from the Dewey Bridge to the overlook of the towers and Professor Valley east of Moab, Utah.

Overleaf — The namesake rock monoliths of the Needles District leap out of the ground at Canyonlands National Park. The sapphire sky and mint-green meadows of Chesler Park provide pleasing contrast to the severe upthrust of rust- and buff-colored stone.

The scenic value of Goblin Valley State Park depends largely on what time of day you arrive. At sundown, shadows define the terrain and enunciate every fold, crack and layer within. The deposits of ancient mud that form the "goblins" take on a distinctive character as the drama of the scene unfolds.

Opposite page — With so many vertical surfaces around, who can resist a full-sized game of shadow puppets as the sun retires? To some, these elongated shadows are suggestive of the mythical Kokopelli of the Hopi tribe. Did the first people to see Goblin Valley indulge the impulse to play in the last light of day?

Thousands of visitors to Island in the Sky see Mesa Arch every year, and photographers at the site are often elbow-to-elbow at sunrise in fair-weather months. Another sort of adventurer appreciates the quiet solitude of the snow-covered scene, at a time when the only car on the road may be your own. If the road isn't snowbound, winter can be an excellent time to see what the summer tourist never will — a landscape draped in white, accentuating and illustrating clearly the division between snow-collecting, horizontal benches and sheer, vertical cliffs.

Out here, you really have to want it. A cowboy maxim applies to flora and fauna alike; if you ain't tough, you ain't gonna make it. Above, a juniper with nowhere to put down roots except a thin fissure in the rock hangs on for dear life.

Yucca plants are exceedingly tough and will thrive in the harshest conditions. Native tribes found myriad uses for the versatile plant. Yucca leaves were used to brew pain-relieving elixirs, and the tough spikes also were used as textiles for clothing and basket-weaving. The roots of the plant were used to make soap and ointments to treat skin ailments. In modern times, the venerable yucca is used most frequently as an ornamental plant in a xeriscape setting.

Just how stable *is* this rock? We thought it best not to stick around long enough to find out, but the prospect of shade on a warm day can dispel thoughts of doom. In the sparsely vegetated creek-bed of Dominguez Canyon, any shelter from the sun seems worth the risk.

Some people are content to admire skyscraper desert towers from afar. Then there are these guys, part of a group of climbers carefully making their way to the corkscrew summit of a formation known as Ancient Art at Fisher Towers, east of Moab, Utah. Upon reaching a reasonably flat platform at the top, this climber felt honor-bound to stand up and strike a pose of victory, if ever so briefly.

A view looking southeast toward Arches National Park just before sunset starkly illustrates the frontier between the gray, green and white world of the Rocky Mountains and the sunburnt desert landscape of the Colorado Plateau. Two distinct scenes, both symbolic of the American West, command the attention of those lucky enough to be passing by.

Here, some of the westernmost sub-ranges of the Rockies lie on the western boundary of the vast uplift of the plateau. These peaks of the La Sal Mountains stand well over 12,000 feet. The terrain falls away nearly 8,000 feet to the Colorado River basin as the river — the lifeblood of the West — winds through the canyons of the Southwest en route to the sea.

Every year, thousands of visitors to Arches National Park make the trip to Delicate Arch, on a 3-mile round-trip over moderately steep slickrock, to see the crown jewel and best-known feature of the park.

This ponderosa pine was spared a grim fate in the Little Park Preserve south of Grand Junction. Because the tree fell against a nearby cliff wall, its roots were left intact and the tree hung on.

Whispering Cave is a popular attraction at Echo Park in Dinosaur National Monument on the Colorado-Utah border. A steady, cool breeze blows through the cave, giving welcome relief on a hot day.

The theropod that left this track in Buckhorn Draw could well be one of the fossils now on display at the Cleveland-Lloyd Dinosaur Quarry in Emery County, Utah. The quarry is the site of one of the richest deposits of Jurassic Period fossils ever found. The unlucky creatures that got stuck in the mud must have looked like an easy meal to larger predators like Allosaurus. When the giant beasts attempted to scavenge the smaller carcasses, they suffered a similar, sticky fate. Many millions of years later, the intermingled bones of predator and prey alike stir the imagination and offer proof that the world we know bears little resemblance to the one these creatures roamed.

These young owls were fascinated to see a human in the back yard of their Grand Junction home.

Bluff, Utah, attracts its fair share of visitors in a busy tourist season. In the winter, the crowds thin out and the small town at the edge of Indian Country needs to work harder to promote itself. Enter the Bluff International Balloon Festival. The balloon glow lights up a midwinter sky, followed the next morning by a mass launch amid the imposing red-rock towers of Valley of the Gods.

The ruins at Butler Wash near Cedar Mesa, Utah, are remarkably intact 800 years after the people who built them vanished. The site dates to 1200 A.D., like much of the development of the Four Corners area that is credited to the Anasazi. The shelter afforded by the cave roof likely made this an enticing bit of real estate in the eyes of its developers, and in turn helped shield the structures from the ravages of water and wind. The ruins are easy to reach on a gentle trail off a rural highway in southern Utah.

Mesa Verde, near Durango, is the crown jewel of archaeological discoveries of the American Southwest. As famous as the site is today, the ruins were unknown to the outside world until 1888.

That year, a rancher named Richard Wetherill spotted Cliff House (pictured) from a nearby mesa. This time capsule of ancient Americans has captured the imaginations of millions since then.

Petroglyphs

The people who lived here before us were not only skilled masons and farmers; some of them spent a considerable amount of time at work on the only recorded "history" of Fremont, Anasazi and Ute cultures. Some of the figures pecked or painted on the rocks are easily recognizable as snakes, deer and bighorn sheep. Others may cause a modern observer to wonder if the ancient inhabitants of this land had been visited by beings from another world.

The pictographs and petroglyphs of Sego Canyon in eastern Utah represent cultures that were separated by thousands of years. This panel is in the Barrier Canyon style and is believed to have been created about 2000 B.C. Art in the archaic style may date back as early as 7000 B.C. As no written language exists to explain these enduring icons, visitors can only imagine what nightmarish visions led to their creation.

Opposite page — These artifacts of an ancient age have lain undisturbed since the inhabitants of Grand Gulch, Utah, abandoned the area, likely being forced out by persistent drought. Centuries after the inhabitants left, this "midden pile" of corncobs can still be found next to the metate used to grind the corn.

Grand Gulch Primitive Area contains a treasure trove of well-preserved ruins and other remnants of the culture that once thrived here. Artifacts from the Basketmaker period in this area date back as early as 200 A.D. During this same time frame half a world away, the Roman Empire stretched from Britain to Syria.

Overleaf— The Dry Fork Canyon Archaeological Site north of Vernal, Utah, is home to a stunning variety of pictographs. The site is on private property, but the owners allow access to visitors as long as they stay on trails and respect the environment and the priceless, timeless art.

Petroglyphs along the Three Kings trail at the McConkie Ranch near Vernal, Utah. The art is attributed to the Fremont culture that flourished in the area before about 1200 A.D. The public is welcome to view the vast gallery of ancient art at the ranch.

A panel of pictographs in Buckhorn Wash, in eastern Utah, is thought to be at least 2,000 years old. The pictographs have been painted onto the rock, which readily absorbed the pigment and allowed the colors to stay vibrant over the ages. The artist likely used hematite, also known as "blood ore," as a coloring agent. What still isn't known is what these figures are meant to represent; some ancient mysteries will likely never be solved.

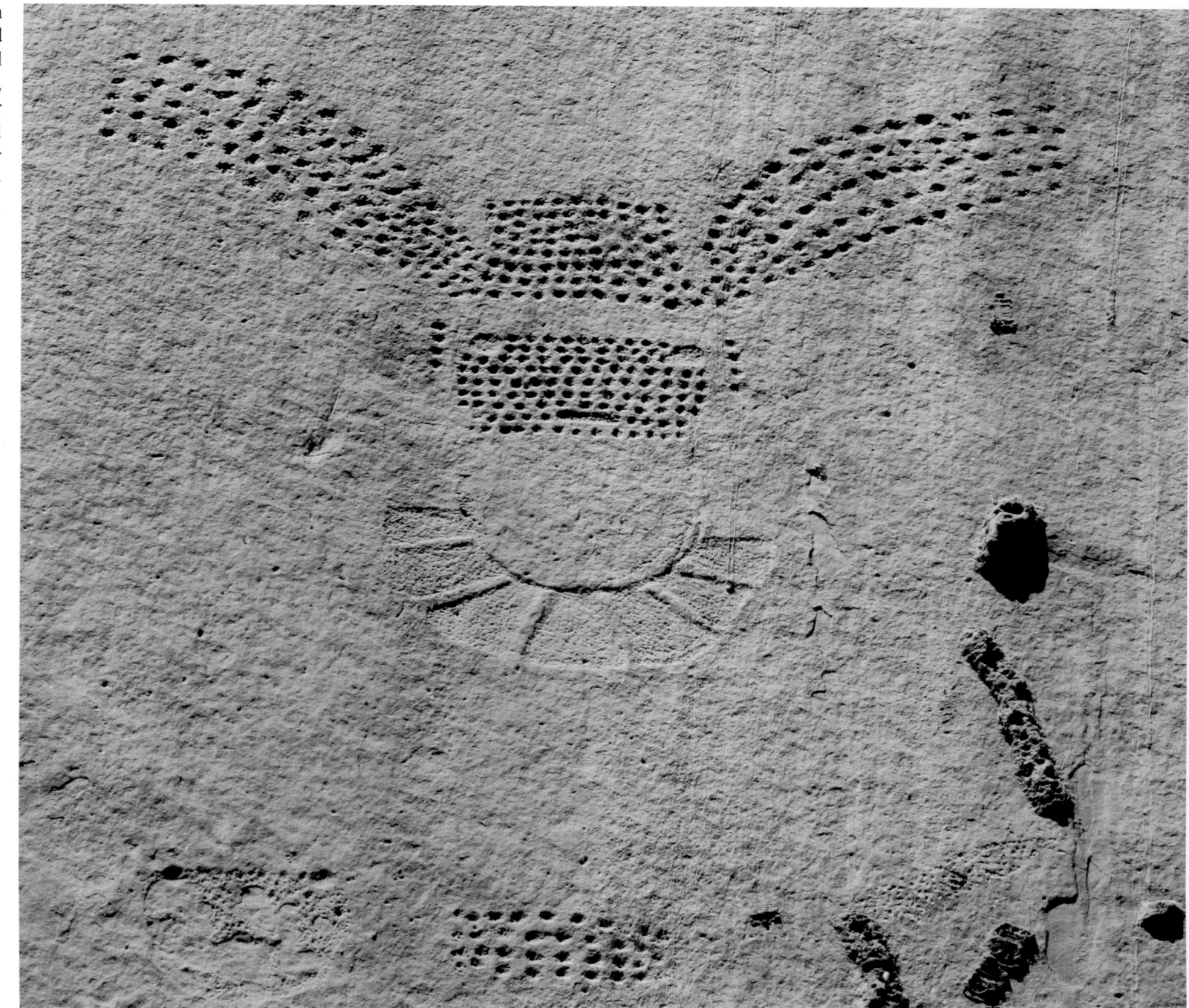

This petroglyph was pecked into a high wall in Echo Park, in Dinosaur National Monument, near the Colorado-Utah border.

The panel known as the Three Kings in Dry Fork Canyon on the McConkie Ranch near Vernal, Utah. The ranch is home to one of the largest and most varied collections of Native American rock art in the West. The petroglyphs and pictographs were etched or drawn on the stone from about 1 A.D. to 1200 A.D. and have weathered the ages with grace and beauty.

One of many petroglyphs carved into the rock in Dry Fork Canyon at the McConkie Ranch site.

Well-preserved ceremonial sites are common throughout Grand Gulch, a remote canyon in southeastern Utah where many artifacts of previous cultures still exist. The area is regarded as sacred by the modern descendants of the Puebloan people who built the structures.

An elaborate panel in Cottonwood Canyon in eastern Utah has come to be known as The Great Hunt. In addition to the many sheep, several hunters are seen to be armed with bows and arrows. This site is near the canyon's junction with the larger Nine Mile Canyon near the town of Wellington, Utah. Nine Mile Canyon contains the richest collection of Native American rock art in North America. There are at least 1,000 documented individual sites, containing upwards of 10,000 individual images. The art has been credited to the Fremont culture and is believed to be about 1,000 years old. Petroglyphs, which have been pecked out of the rock, are at much less risk of erosion and degradation than the painted pictographs, which are perpetually at the mercy of sun, wind and water.

The ruins at Hovenweep National Monument aren't believed to have been any type of dwelling for the people who built them. Like many of the artifacts left behind, however, there is still an aura of mystery about these structures. Whether they were used for spiritual rites, or more worldly concerns such as storage of perishable goods, is left to the imaginations of those who stop to ponder.

The rock art that adorns the walls of Nine Mile Canyon is so extensive, the area has come to be thought of as an outdoor gallery. Scientists and laymen alike marvel at the art's durability, and its recurring themes and styles. After years of analysis, the most fundamental questions are still unanswered: who carved these glyphs and why? The art is attributed to the Fremont people who lived in the area from about 600 A.D. to 1400 A.D., but practically nothing is known about the artists' impetus and inspiration for the painstaking creations.

Mountains

Colorado is practically synonymous with the Rocky Mountains — the "spine" of the continent splits the state from north to south. Colorado boasts the tallest mountains in the Rockies, with 54 of its peaks rising above 14,000 feet, hundreds more that top out above 13,000 feet, and still hundreds more that rise above timberline at about 12,000 feet. No other state's identity is so closely bound to its own rugged terrain as Colorado — the roof of the Rockies.

Opposite page — Mount Sneffels, seen from Dallas Divide above the town of Ridgway, appears to be divided between seasons as its rugged north face already is wearing its white winter cloak. A few miles to the north of the summit and thousands of feet below, aspen trees have only just begun their transformation from summer green to autumn gold.

Colorado's mountain basins, covered in snow much of the year, become a showcase of floral beauty in summer. The centerpiece of every arrangement is the Rocky Mountain Columbine, Colorado's state flower. Uprooting columbines is forbidden by state law, and only 25 blossoms may be gathered in a day.

A lazy, meandering creek becomes a ribbon-like waterfall near Lands End Road on Grand Mesa. The creek cuts through meadows in a channel no wider than an irrigation ditch in places, then plunges off the eastern edge of the mesa in a spectacular, misty drop. Several similar waterfalls are hidden among the lodgepole and fir pines on the eastern edge of the flat-topped mountain.

Opposite page — Dave takes in a 360-degree panorama from the top of Mount Sneffels, the 14,150-foot "Queen of the San Juans." Most people who climb Sneffels approach it from Yankee Boy Basin to the south.

Most aspen trees in Colorado turn yellow and gold in autumn, but a spectacular few, under the right conditions, can produce more vivid oranges, reds and purples.

A stand of aspens on Piñon Mesa southwest of Grand Junction puts on a dazzling display of color. The color of the leaves can vary dramatically, depending on weather conditions and the trees' genetics. When compounds known as anthocyanins are abundant in the plant, aspen leaves turn strikingly red.

On Piñon Mesa, a random turn down a dirt road might deposit a traveler onto a bench overlooking an aspen-filled valley. Evergreens and rust-colored oak brush provide the accent colors to the vibrant fall scene.

Overleaf — Piñon Mesa would be the northern edge of the Uncompahgre Plateau had it not been neatly cleaved from the plateau by the deep fissure of Unaweep Canyon.

As travelers leave Montrose and travel south on U.S. Highway 550, the dominant feature on the horizon grows larger and more impressive by the mile. Traveling southwest from the town of Ridgway on Colorado Highway 62, Mount Sneffels is such a commanding presence, cars often line the road while their occupants stop to gawk. A well-worn wide spot near the summit of Dallas Divide allows the awestruck to safely pull over and enjoy the majesty of the landscape.

Twin Falls, in Yankee Boy Basin near Ouray, offers proof that if one soul-soothing waterfall is a good thing, two is twice as nice. In late summer, the basin is filled with wildflowers of all descriptions, adding to its considerable charm. Jeepers, hikers, climbers, wildlife watchers, cloud-shape evaluators and lotus eaters all gather here with equal enthusiasm. The area was once an epicenter of precious-metal mining in southwestern Colorado. Today, the wild beauty of the basin represents something more valuable than silver and gold.

Opposite page — Yankee Boy Basin gets more than its share of visitors in the summer. By the time the snow falls and the road into the basin becomes difficult to travel, only the hardiest adventurers are willing to make the trip. The basin is a profusion of color and life in the brief alpine summer; the landscape is transformed entirely in the harsh beauty of winter.

Potosi Peak stands guard over a landscape draped in white, abandoned by all but a few intrepid souls on a winter's day. By only a few hundred feet, the 13,786-foot peak near Ouray barely misses being one of Colorado's more challenging Fourteener climbs.

Yellow daisies intermingle with great spikes of purple lupine on Piñon Mesa.

Daisy fleabane are found in great numbers on Grand Mesa and other high-elevation settings.

Indian paintbrush do well in both desert and alpine settings. This specimen on Piñon Mesa feels right at home alongside other varieties of flowers more commonly found at higher elevations.

Can't see the forest for the trees? Try looking straight up. These strikingly tall aspens near Owl Creek Pass may make you forget all about the twinge in your neck.

Sometimes the wildlife comes to visit the valleys down below. This bear was seen perched in a cottonwood tree in Grand Junction. When their natural food sources run low in the mountains, bears will roam many miles to find a meal. This leads to an unfortunate outcome for a bear that makes a nuisance of itself once it learns to associate food with the presence of humans.

Once hunted to near extinction in the early 20th century, elk have rebounded and large herds now populate the Rocky Mountains. Elk are also known as "wapiti," the name used by Native Americans. Elk are the largest of the deer family and can grow to weigh as much as half a ton.

On Owl Creek Pass, between the towns of Cimarron and Ridgway, the weather had been slightly less than cooperative en route to camp. A soaking rain gave way to blinding sunlight within a few moments, and a spectacular rainbow appeared over the East Fork of the Cimarron River. A view of the rainbow is captured with a wide-angle lens in the scene above.

The same rainbow is recorded in vivid detail, this time with a telephoto lens. The right amount of water vapor in the air, the sun at the perfect angle in the sky and a dark backdrop for contrast provided the perfect conditions for this visual treat to appear.

An artist's palette of colors greets sturdy hikers on a ridge far above Lake Irwin, near the town of Crested Butte. The view from the ridge reveals that even though they are hours apart by highway travel, the towns of Aspen and Crested Butte are within walking distance of each other. What lies between is some of the most inspiring scenic wilderness in Colorado.

As autumn takes over the meadows and glades, winter tightens its grip on the forbidding north face of the Sneffels Range as seen from Dallas Divide near the town of Ridgway. With the green grass of summer hanging on for dear life on the valley floor, a passerby who stops to ponder the majesty of the scene may have the sensation of experiencing three different seasons in one day.

Water

Most of the surface of the Earth is covered in water, yet only a tiny fraction of that is fresh water. Yesterday's cloud becomes today's raindrop and falls to the ground, where nature compels it to return to the sea, in an endless cycle as old as the planet. Water, in the arid West, does more than make life possible; it makes *quality* of life possible.

Opposite page — The famous Maroon Bells might be the most photographed mountains in Colorado. On a cool fall morning, with the glassy surface of Crater Lake as a mirror, a lucky visitor gets two views in one.

A streambed filled with fresh rainwater, accompanied by a sunlit scene in the background, is a photographer's dream in Mee Canyon in McInnis Canyons National Conservation Area.

Spring is slow to arrive on top of Grand Mesa. When the Grand Valley below is greening up and warming to a new season, the last vestiges of winter cling to the lake shores and shady pine forests.

On an average day, the temperature on top of the world's largest flat-topped mountain can be 20-25 degrees cooler than the valley floor some 5,000 feet below.

On a frosty day in Grand Junction, an ice-fisherman had brought his son with him to a frozen Corn Lake. The fisherman got a strike and pulled a small trout from a hole in the ice. "Watch this," he told his son as he flipped the fish onto the frozen surface. A great blue heron waiting nearby wasted no time collecting the easiest meal of his life.

A blue heron takes wing at the Lucy Ferril Ela Wildlife Sanctuary near Connected Lakes in Grand Junction. With so much water nearby in the form of lakes and rivers, many species of birds are frequent visitors to the sanctuary.

Overleaf — Connected Lakes on the stillest of October days. With even a hint of a breeze, the surface of the water would ripple and distort the scene. This day, however, was a day for quiet reflection.

Duke Lake is a scene of tranquility during the last light of day at Connected Lakes State Park.

A pool of water after a desert rain is a fleeting, ephemeral thing. Any of the maze of slot canyons south of Grand Junction can harbor such pools for days or even weeks, protecting them from harsh, drying sunlight with steep canyon walls.

A bald eagle searches some of the last remaining unfrozen shoreline near the dam of Blue Mesa Reservoir as winter sets in. The reservoir, west of the town of Gunnison, will have entirely frozen over before the end of the season, situated in a high valley that routinely gets some of the most frigid winter weather of anywhere in the continental United States.

In late autumn, after the first snows but before Maroon Creek Road has closed for winter, a sightseer stands a fair chance of enjoying relative solitude. In fair-weather months, Maroon Lake (foreground) draws heavy tourist traffic. Because of the steady rise in visitation, the U.S. Forest Service has instituted a shuttle service for visitors to experience one of Colorado's most iconic and well-loved scenes.

Ducks find wintertime in the Grand Valley to their liking. The ducks will travel as far as they need to in order to find suitable winter weather, and the Colorado and Gunnison river basins and numerous lakes and ponds in western Colorado are favorite stops.

Millions of people have visited Delicate Arch, the premier attraction at Arches National Park in eastern Utah. Few of them venture off the well-beaten trail to explore other hidden treasures, and fewer still see the arch reflected in the undulating patterns of a snowmelt pond.

If the town of Ridgway didn't already have enough scenic attractions, the annual spring hot-air balloon festival would guarantee another splash of vivid color. The launch takes place at Ridgway Reservoir and is accentuated by the dramatic light of early morning.

The bright magenta blooms of Parry's primrose grace the summertime streambanks of the San Juan Mountains. If the columbine hadn't been picked for Colorado's state flower, Parry's primrose may well have earned the honor. This show-off is a mainstay of the alpine wetlands of the San Juans and provides striking contrast to the variegated greens of the high country.

In the spring of 1997, Comet Hale-Bopp blazed across the sky every night. Chris says: "I knew the shot I wanted, but it took awhile to find an arch that framed the comet the way I wanted. I found what I was looking for at Turret Arch in Arches National Park. I opened the shutter and walked around the base of the arch, hitting the rock with my flash. A photo like this comes once in a lifetime."

Night sky

The American West is famous for its stunning scenery, but if you're only looking in the bright light of day you're missing half the show. Far from city lights, and with a combination of high elevation and clear, dry air is a stellar sprawl that helps put our universe in context. In this way and many others, the West is blessed.

A tripod and a shutter cable were used to create this scene at a campsite in east-central Utah. The shutter was left open for a few minutes and a flashlight was used to "paint" the foreground with light. The brilliant stars of the Milky Way galaxy and the rosy glow of a campfire add extra illumination to the striking scene.

Opposite page —
A pond above Lake Irwin, near Crested Butte, reflects a fiery sunset off its mirrorlike surface.

The same pond above Lake Irwin puts on a different face after sundown. At about 10,000 feet in elevation, and with no light pollution from nearby cities, the night sky glitters with diamond dust. In summer, the thick cloud of stars at the edge of the Milky Way galaxy looms overhead.

A closer look at the moon, courtesy of a telephoto lens, reveals a pock-marked and scarred surface. Over eons, the lunar surface has taken uncountable, cataclysmic hits from asteroids. The Tycho crater, visible at bottom center in this frame, was caused by just such an impact. Because the moon has no atmosphere — and no wind or water erosion — the crater's appearance has not changed.

A crescent moon, pulled in tight with a telephoto lens, looks as though it may have been photographed from a passing spacecraft. In fact, even an earthbound photographer can capture this scene if the proper equipment is used. With the moon in a crescent phase, sunlight streams in from an oblique angle, accentuating the contours and giving depth to the craters that cover the lunar surface.

On June 5, 2012, the planet Venus upstaged the sun for the second time this century. As the sun and its dark companion dropped behind the Colorado Plateau, they descended into the haze of smoke from a nearby wildfire. The smoke acted as a filter and deepened the red-orange sunset. If you missed this transit of Venus, take heart; the next one will take place Dec. 10, 2117.

The shoreline of a pond in a residential subdivision in Grand Junction is decorated with lights for Christmas every year. The naturally occurring decorations that stop people in their tracks, however, aren't as predictable, and are arguably more valuable because of that fact.

Only part of the waxing-crescent moon gets direct sunlight, but even the shaded area can be seen because of Earthshine reflecting onto the lunar surface. Poetically put, this is called "the new moon in the old moon's arms."

A small aperture, fast shutter speed and heavy filter were used to show the moon encroaching on the sun during an annular eclipse on May 20, 2012. This scene was recorded at Lake Powell just before the moon positioned itself directly in front of the sun.

Usually a photographer relies on skill, but sometimes success comes down to dumb luck. This awe-inspiring display of the Northern Lights surprised and delighted campers at Utah's Goblin Valley in the spring of 2001. The aurora borealis, normally associated with northern latitudes, can be seen far to the south during intense solar storms that bombard Earth's magnetic poles with charged particles. Says Chris: "I had no idea how long the exposure should be, or if anything would show up at all." Because the frames were shot on film he couldn't immediately develop, Chris didn't know for several days whether he had captured the vivid scene. Happily for him, and for us, he did.

Light from a campfire illuminates the rocks in the Utah desert as the stars appear to swirl overhead. The apparent rotation of stars is imperceptibly slow to the human eye, but a long exposure clearly illustrates the path of the stars as they describe a circle around the north celestial pole. Observers in the northern hemisphere use Polaris — the North Star — as the nearest reference to this point on the celestial sphere.

Opposite page — Streaks of stars complement the glow of a fire and the lanterns of campers hiking along a ledge in Grand County, Utah. The longer the exposure, the longer the star trails appear to be in the frame.